◖SCHOLASTIC

File-Folder Games *in COLOR*

Numbers & Counting

by Susan Julio

New York • Toronto • London • Auckland • Sydney
Mexico City • New Delhi • Hong Kong • Buenos Aires

Teaching *Resources*

Cover design by Jason Robinson
Interior design by Solas
Cover and interior illustrations by Rusty Fletcher

ISBN 978-0-439-46592-2

Contents

File-Folder Games

About This Book

File-Folder Games in Color: Numbers & Counting offers an engaging and fun way to motivate children of all learning styles and help build their number knowledge. Research shows that knowing and understanding numbers is fundamental in developing more advanced math skills. In addition, the games in this book will help children meet important math standards. (See What the Research Says and Meeting the Math Standards, page 6, for more.)

The games are a snap to set up and store: Just tear out the full-color game boards from this book, glue them inside file folders, and you've got ten instant learning center activities. Children will have fun as they practice counting to ten with Counting Sheep, matching numbers to sets with The Cat's Pajamas, adding one in Hippo Hurdles, skip-counting by twos in Leap Frog, and much more.

What's Inside

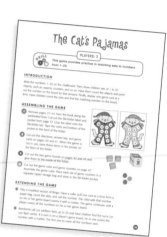

Each game includes the following:

- an introductory page for the teacher that provides a suggestion for introducing the game

- step-by-step assembly directions

- Extending the Game activities to continue reinforcing children's skills and interest

- a label with the title of each game for the file-folder tab

- a pocket to attach to the front of the file folder for storing the game parts

- directions that explain to children how to play the game

- an answer key

- game cards

- one or more game boards

- some games also include game markers, game counters, and a game cube or spinner

Making the File-Folder Games

In addition to the game pages, you will need the following:

- 10 file folders (in a variety of colors, if possible)
- scissors
- clear packing tape
- glue stick or rubber cement
- paper clips
- brass fasteners

Tips

- Back the spinners, game cubes, and game markers with tagboard before assembling. Laminate for durability.

- Before cutting apart the game cards, make additional copies (in color or black and white) for use with the Extending the Game activities.

- Place the accessories for each game, such as spinners, game cubes, game counters, and game markers in separate, labeled zipper storage bags. Keep the bags in a basket near the games.

Using the File-Folder Games

- Before introducing the games to children, conduct mini-lessons to review the numbers and math concept used in each game.

- Model how to play each game. You might also play it with children the first time.

- Give children suggestions on how to determine the order in which players take turns, such as rolling a die and taking turns in numerical order.

- Store the games in a math center and encourage children to play in pairs or small groups before or after school, during free-choice time, or when they have finished other tasks.

- Send the games home for children to play with family members and friends.

- Use the Extending the Game activities to continue reinforcing children's skills and interest.

Storage Ideas

Keep the file-folder games in any of these places:

- math center
- vertical file tray
- file box
- file cabinet
- bookshelf
- plastic stacking crate

What the Research Says

Number is central to our mathematics curriculum. NCTM, in its *Principles and Standards for School Mathematics* (2000), stresses the importance of attaining "a rich understanding of numbers—what they are; how they are represented with objects, numerals, or on number lines; how they are related to one another; how numbers are embedded in systems that have structures and properties; and how to use numbers and operations to solve problems." Learning numbers and what they represent is critical for early mathematical development and is essential for understanding operations and developing computational fluency.

Meeting the Math Standards

Connections to the McREL Math Standards

Mid-continent Research for Education and Learning (McREL), a nationally recognized, nonprofit organization, has compiled and evaluated national and state standards—and proposed what teachers should provide for their PreK–K students to grow proficient in math. This book's games and activities support the following standards:

Understands and applies basic and advanced properties of the concepts of numbers including:

- Understands that numbers are symbols used to represent the quantity of objects
- Counts by ones to ten or higher
- Understands one-to-one correspondence
- Understands symbolic, concrete, and pictorial representations of numbers (e.g., written numerals, objects in sets)
- Understands the concept of position in a sequence
- Counts whole numbers (cardinal and ordinal numbers)
- Knows the written numerals 0–9
- Understands basic whole number relationships (e.g., 4 is less than 10)

Uses basic and advanced procedures while performing the processes of computation including:

- Knows that the quantity of objects can change by adding or taking away objects
- Adds whole numbers

Source: Kendall, J. S. & Marzano, R. J. (2004). *Content knowledge: A compendium of standards and benchmarks for K–12 education.* Aurora, CO: Mid-continent Research for Education and Learning. Online database: http://www.mcrel.org/standards-benchmarks/

Connections to the NCTM Math Standards

The activities in this book are also designed to support you in meeting the following PreK–K standards recommended by the National Council of Teachers of Mathematics (NCTM) for Number and Operations:

Understand numbers, ways of representing numbers, relationships among numbers, and number systems:

- Count with understanding and recognize "how many" in sets of objects
- Develop understanding of the relative position and magnitude of whole numbers and of ordinal and cardinal numbers and their connections
- Develop a sense of whole numbers and represent and use them in flexible ways, including relating and composing numbers
- Connect number words and numerals to the quantities they represent

Source: National Council of Teachers of Mathematics. (2000). *Principles and Standards for School Mathematics.* Reston, VA: NCTM. www.nctm.org

Counting Sheep

PLAYERS: 2

SKILL

This game provides practice in counting objects from 1–10.

INTRODUCTION

Display ten sheep counters from the game. Chorally count to ten with children, pointing to one counter at a time as you go along. Then call out different numbers between 1–10. Invite volunteers to count the sheep, one-by-one, up to each named number.

ASSEMBLING THE GAME

1 Remove pages 9–19 from the book along the perforated lines. Cut out the file-folder label and pocket from page 9. Glue the label onto the file-folder tab. Tape the sides and bottom of the pocket to the front of the folder.

2 Cut out the directions, answer key, and game cards on pages 11 and 13. When the game is not in use, store these items in the pocket on the front of the folder.

3 Cut out the two game boards on pages 15 and 17 and glue them to the inside of the folder.

4 Cut out the game cube and game counters on page 19. Assemble the game cube. Place each set of counters in a separate zipper storage bag and store in the file-folder pocket.

EXTENDING THE GAME

◎ Use a wipe-off pen to write a number from 1–10 on a set of ten sheep counters in each color. Then have children sequence the counters on their game boards.

◎ Make up simple word problems for children to solve. For instance, say, "Two sheep were in the meadow. Three more sheep joined them. How many sheep are in the meadow now?" Have children use the counters and game board to show how they get their answer.

Counting Sheep

GET READY TO PLAY

- Each player chooses a game board and a set of 12 sheep counters.
- Shuffle the number cards. Place them facedown.

TO PLAY

1 Roll the game cube. Take the number of cards shown on the cube.

2 Look at the number on each card. Count out that many sheep onto your game board. Each time, check your answer on the answer key. Did you count the correct number of sheep?

- If so, keep the number card.
- If not, put the card on the bottom of the stack.

3 After each turn, take the sheep counters off your game board.

4 Keep taking turns. Play continues until all the cards have been used. The player with the most cards wins the game.

Counting Sheep

ANSWER KEY

1

2

3

4

5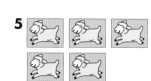

6

7

8

9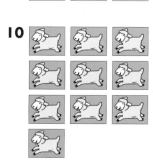

10

1	2	3	4
5	6	7	8
9	10	1	2
3	4	5	6
7	8	9	10

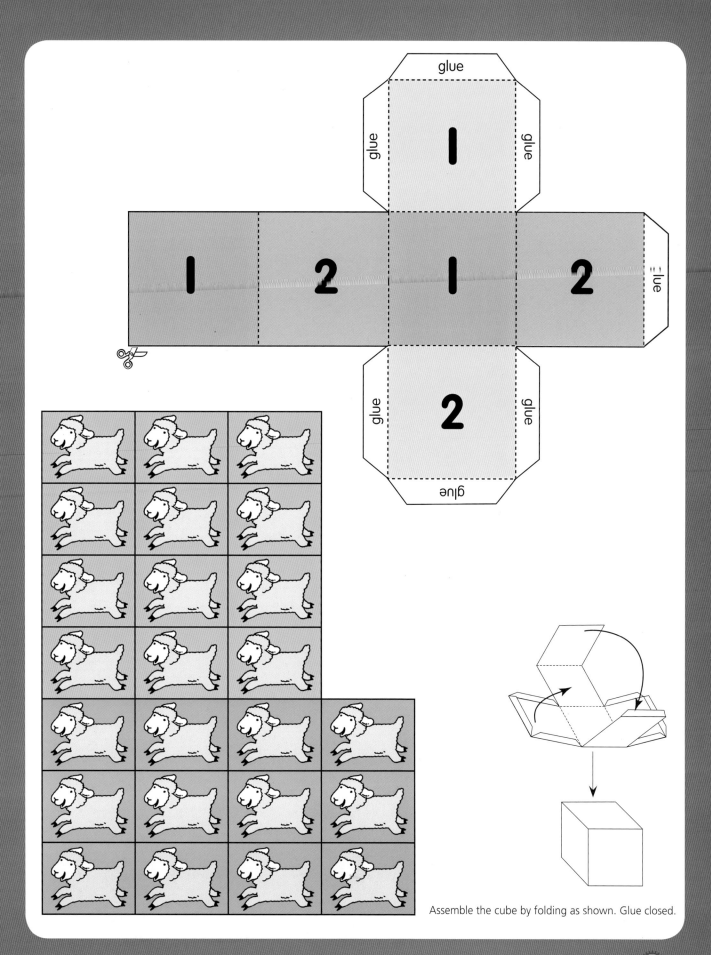

Assemble the cube by folding as shown. Glue closed.

Hungry Hogs

PLAYERS: 2-3

 SKILL

This game provides practice in recognizing numbers from 1–20.

INTRODUCTION

Display the number cards from the game. Name a number and ask a volunteer to point out the matching card. Repeat until each number from 1–20 has been identified.

ASSEMBLING THE GAME

1 Remove pages 23–33 from the book along the perforated lines. Cut out the file-folder label and pocket from page 23. Glue the label onto the file-folder tab. Tape the sides and bottom of the pocket to the front of the folder.

2 Cut out the directions, answer key, and game cards on pages 25 and 27. When the game is not in use, store these items in the pocket on the front of the folder.

3 Cut out the two sides of the game board on pages 29 and 31 and glue them to the inside of the folder.

4 Cut out and assemble the game cube and game markers on page 33.

EXTENDING THE GAME

◎ Make a duplicate set of number cards. Then invite children to use 10 pairs of matching cards to play Memory.

◎ Place the number cards in a paper bag. Have children take turns drawing two numbers from the bag, reading the numbers, and telling which one is the highest (or lowest).

Hungry Hogs

Hungry Hogs

GET READY TO PLAY

- Each player places a game marker on Start.
- Shuffle the cards. Stack them facedown on the game board.

TO PLAY

1 Take the top card and read the number.
Did you say the correct number?

- If so, roll the cube and move ahead
  to the first space in that color.
- If not, your turn ends.

2 After each turn, place the card on the bottom of the stack.

3 Keep taking turns. The first player to reach Finish wins the game.

PLAYING TIPS

- Players may land on and share the same space.
- Players must roll the matching color to move to Finish.

Hungry Hogs

ANSWER KEY

1 (one)	11 (eleven)
2 (two)	12 (twelve)
3 (three)	13 (thirteen)
4 (four)	14 (fourteen)
5 (five)	15 (fifteen)
6 (six)	16 (sixteen)
7 (seven)	17 (seventeen)
8 (eight)	18 (eighteen)
9 (nine)	19 (nineteen)
10 (ten)	20 (twenty)

1	2	3	4
5	6	7	8
9	10	11	12
13	14	15	16
17	18	19	20

Start

Cut along this edge and attach to page 31.

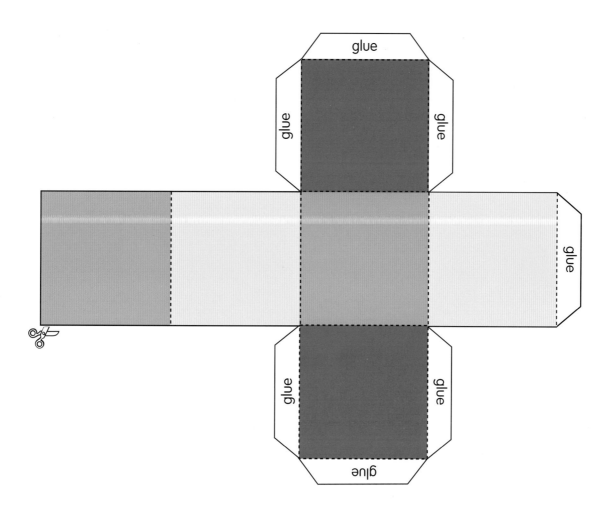

Fold the tabs on the game markers
so they stand up.

Fold here.

Fold here.

Fold here.

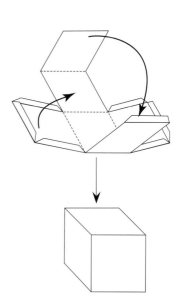

Assemble the cube by folding as shown. Glue closed.

The Cat's Pajamas

PLAYERS: 2

INTRODUCTION

Write the numbers 1–20 on the chalkboard. Then show children sets of 1 to 20 objects, such as crayons, counters, and so on. Have them count the objects and point out the number on the board for that amount. Finally, display one game card at a time. Have children count the dots and find the matching number on the board.

ASSEMBLING THE GAME

1. Remove pages 37–47 from the book along the perforated lines. Cut out the file-folder label and pocket from page 37. Glue the label onto the file-folder tab. Tape the sides and bottom of the pocket to the front of the folder.

2. Cut out the directions, answer key, and game cards on pages 39 and 41. When the game is not in use, store these items in the pocket on the front of the folder.

3. Cut out the two game boards on pages 43 and 45 and glue them to the inside of the folder.

4. Cut out the game cube and game counters on page 47. Assemble the game cube. Place each set of game counters in a separate zipper storage bag and store in the file-folder pocket.

EXTENDING THE GAME

◎ Play a modified version of Bingo. Have a caller pull one card at a time from a paper bag, count the dots, and call the number. The child with that number on his or her game board covers it with a marker. The game continues until a player covers all the numbers on his or her game board.

◎ Randomly call out addition facts up to 20 and have children find the sums (or use flash cards). If a sum is on a player's game board, he or she covers the number with a marker. The first one to cover all the numbers wins.

The Cat's Pajamas

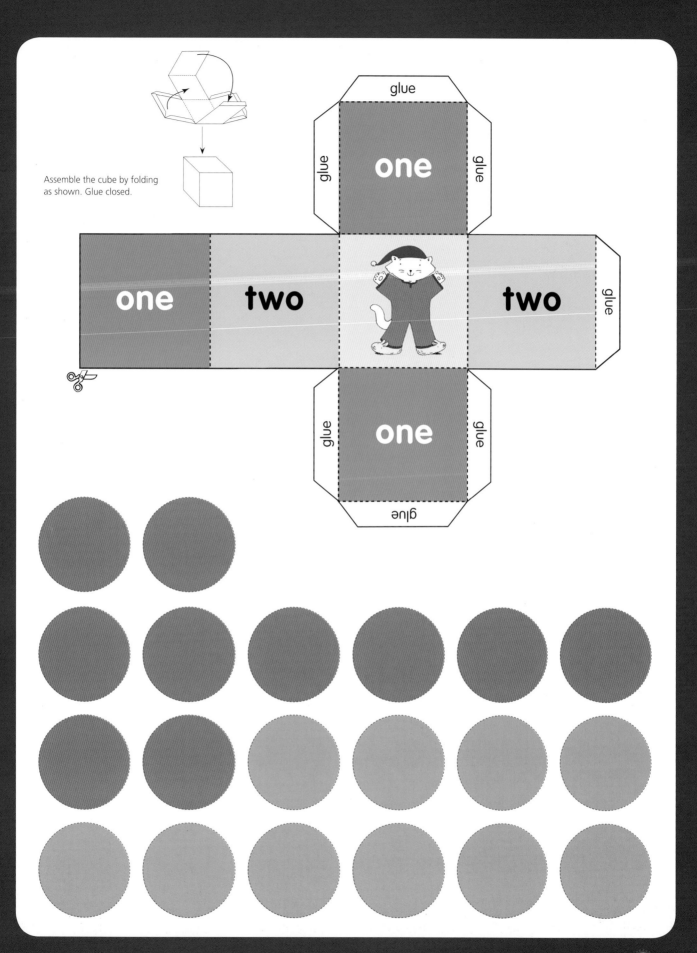

Assemble the cube by folding as shown. Glue closed.

glue
glue one glue
one two two glue
glue one glue
glue

Apple-Seed Number Sentences

PLAYERS: 2

This game provides practice in creating number comparison sentences using numbers 1–9.

INTRODUCTION

Review the meaning of the signs for greater than (>), less than (<), and equal to (=). Then name pairs of numbers between 1 and 9. For each pair, have children tell whether the first number is greater than, less than, or equal to the second number. Help them write a number comparison sentence on the chalkboard.

ASSEMBLING THE GAME

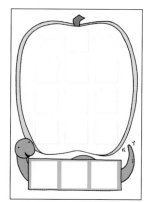
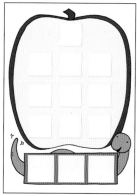

1. Remove pages 51–61 from the book along the perforated lines. Cut out the file-folder label and pocket from page 51. Glue the label onto the file-folder tab. Tape the sides and bottom of the pocket to the front of the folder.

2. Cut out the directions and answer key on page 53. When the game is not in use, store these items in the pocket on the front of the folder.

3. Cut out the two game boards on pages 55 and 57 and glue them to the inside of the folder.

4. Cut out the game cubes and game counters on pages 59 and 61. Assemble the game cubes. Place each set of game counters in a separate zipper storage bag and store in the file-folder pocket.

EXTENDING THE GAME

◎ Copy and cut out two sets of the apple-seed counters for each player. Use a different color of paper for each set. After players set up a number comparison sentence, have them check it by counting out the corresponding number of apple seeds for each side of the sentence.

◎ To provide more numbers to compare, trim sticky notes to fit the sides of the number cubes. Then write numbers from 1–20 on the notes and attach them to the cubes. Have children use these modified cubes to play the game.

Apple-Seed Number Sentences

Apple-Seed Number Sentences

GET READY TO PLAY

Each player chooses a game board and takes a set of 10 apple-seed counters.

TO PLAY

1 Roll the three game cubes. Look at the sign and numbers they land on. Can you make a true number sentence with the sign and numbers?

• If so, place the cubes in the box to show your number sentence. Then put an apple seed on your game board.

• If not, your turn ends.

2 After each turn, check the answer key. Is your answer correct? If not, take the apple seed off the game board.

3 Keep taking turns. The first player to use all of his or her apple seeds wins the game.

Apple-Seed Number Sentences

ANSWER KEY

Is Greater Than (>)			Is Less Than (<)			Is Equal To (=)
9 > 6	7 > 6	5 > 4	1 < 4	3 < 4	5 < 6	4 = 4
9 > 5	7 > 5	5 > 3	1 < 5	3 < 5	5 < 7	5 = 5
9 > 4	7 > 4	5 > 2	1 < 6	3 < 6	5 < 8	6 = 6
9 > 3	7 > 3	5 > 1	1 < 7	3 < 7	5 < 9	
9 > 2	7 > 2	4 > 3	1 < 8	3 < 8	6 < 7	
9 > 1	7 > 1	4 > 2	1 < 9	3 < 9	6 < 8	
8 > 6	6 > 5	4 > 1	2 < 4	4 < 5	6 < 9	
8 > 5	6 > 4		2 < 5	4 < 6		
8 > 4	6 > 3		2 < 6	4 < 7		
8 > 3	6 > 2		2 < 7	4 < 8		
8 > 2	6 > 1		2 < 8	4 < 9		
8 > 1			2 < 9			

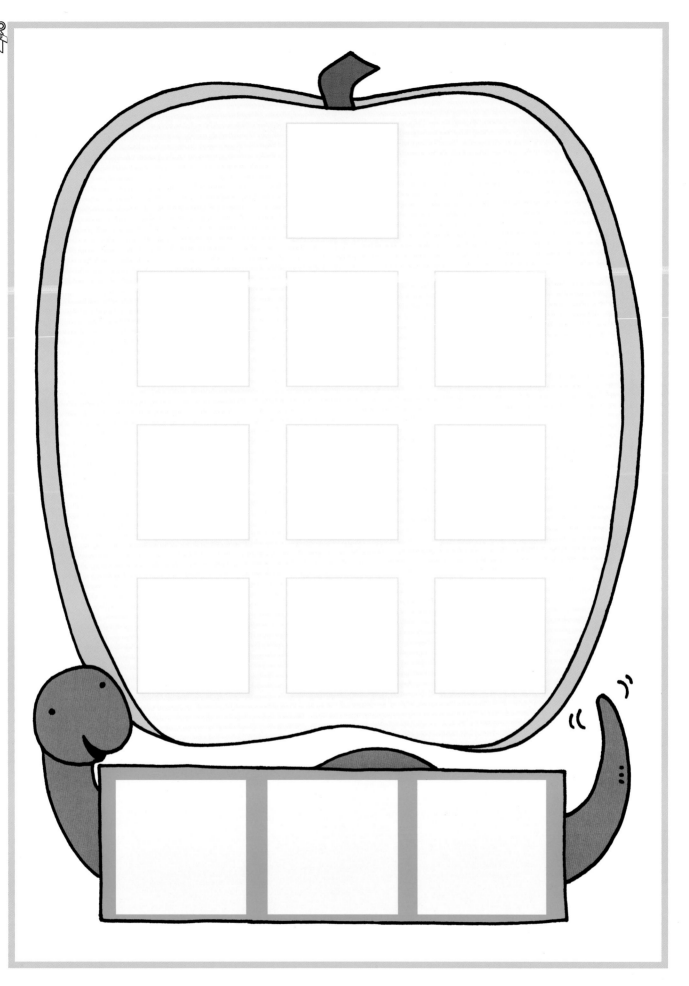

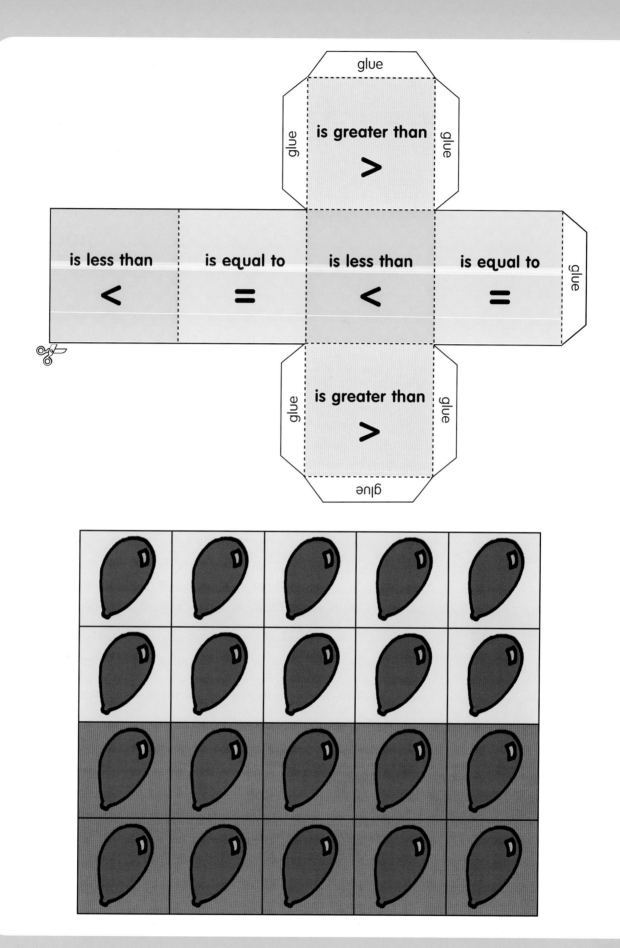

BATTING PRACTICE

Batting Practice

GET READY TO PLAY

- Each player chooses a team and the matching game marker. Place each marker on any yellow base on the game board.

- Shuffle the cards. Stack them facedown on the game board.

TO PLAY

1 Roll the cube. Move that number of spaces. Follow the directions on the space.

2 If the space has a bat, take a card. Read the number. Does it match a number in the top box on your team's side?
- If so, place the card on the box.
- If not, put the card on the bottom of the stack.

3 After each turn, check the answer key. Is your answer correct? If not, put the card on the bottom of the stack

4 Keep taking turns. Cover the boxes for your team in order from top to bottom. The first player to cover all of his or her boxes wins the game.

PLAYING TIPS

- Players may land on and share the same space.

- Players may place only one card on each of their team's boxes.

Batting Practice

ANSWER KEY

1	5	9	13	17
2	6	10	14	18
3	7	11	15	19
4	8	12	16	20

TEAM A

1 2 3 4

5 6 7 8

9 10 11 12

13 14 15 16

17 18 19 20

Go ahead 1.

Go back 1.

CA

Cut along this edge and attach to page 73.

TEAM B

Skip a turn.

Go ahead 1.

Go again.

RDS

	1
	2
	3
	4

	5
	6
	7
	8

	9
	10
	11
	12

	13
	14
	15
	16

	17
	18
	19
	20

Hippo Hurdles

SKILL This game provides practice in adding 1 to numbers from 0–19.

INTRODUCTION

To give children practice in adding 1, show them one game card at a time. Have them name the number. Then invite a volunteer to add 1 to the number and tell the sum.

ASSEMBLING THE GAME

1 Remove pages 79–89 from the book along the perforated lines. Cut out the file-folder label and pocket from page 79. Glue the label onto the file-folder tab. Tape the sides and bottom of the pocket to the front of the folder.

2 Cut out the directions, answer key, and game cards on pages 81 and 83. When the game is not in use, store these items in the pocket on the front of the folder.

3 Cut out the two sides of the game board on pages 85 and 87 and glue them to the inside of the folder.

4 Cut out and assemble the game cube and game markers on page 89.

EXTENDING THE GAME

◎ Duplicate the game cards and place each set in separate paper bags. Give the bags to two teams for a relay. On a signal, each team passes the bag from player to player. On his or her turn, the player draws a card, adds 1 to the number, and tells the sum—before passing the bag to the next player. The first team to empty its bag and give all the correct sums wins the relay.

◎ To further challenge children, invite them to draw a game card from the bag, add 2 to the number, and tell the sum. Later, you might have them add by other increments, such as 3, 4, or even 10!

Hippo Hurdles

GET READY TO PLAY

- Each player places a game marker on Start.
- Shuffle the cards. Stack them facedown on the game board.

TO PLAY

1 Roll the cube. Count the shoes and move that number of spaces. Follow the directions on the space.

2 If the space has a +1 on it, take a card. Read the number. Then add 1 to the number and tell your answer.

3 Check the answer key. Is your answer correct?
- If so, leave your marker on the space.
- If not, move your marker back to where it was.

4 Keep taking turns. The first player to reach Finish wins the game.

PLAYING TIPS

- Players may land on and share the same space.
- Players put the card on the bottom of the stack at the end of each turn.

Hippo Hurdles

ANSWER KEY

0 + 1 = 1	7 + 1 = 8	14 + 1 = 15
1 + 1 = 2	8 + 1 = 9	15 + 1 = 16
2 + 1 = 3	9 + 1 = 10	16 + 1 = 17
3 + 1 = 4	10 + 1 = 11	17 + 1 = 18
4 + 1 = 5	11 + 1 = 12	18 + 1 = 19
5 + 1 = 6	12 + 1 = 13	19 + 1 = 20
6 + 1 = 7	13 + 1 = 14	

0	1	2	3
4	5	6	7
8	9	10	11
12	13	14	15
16	17	18	19

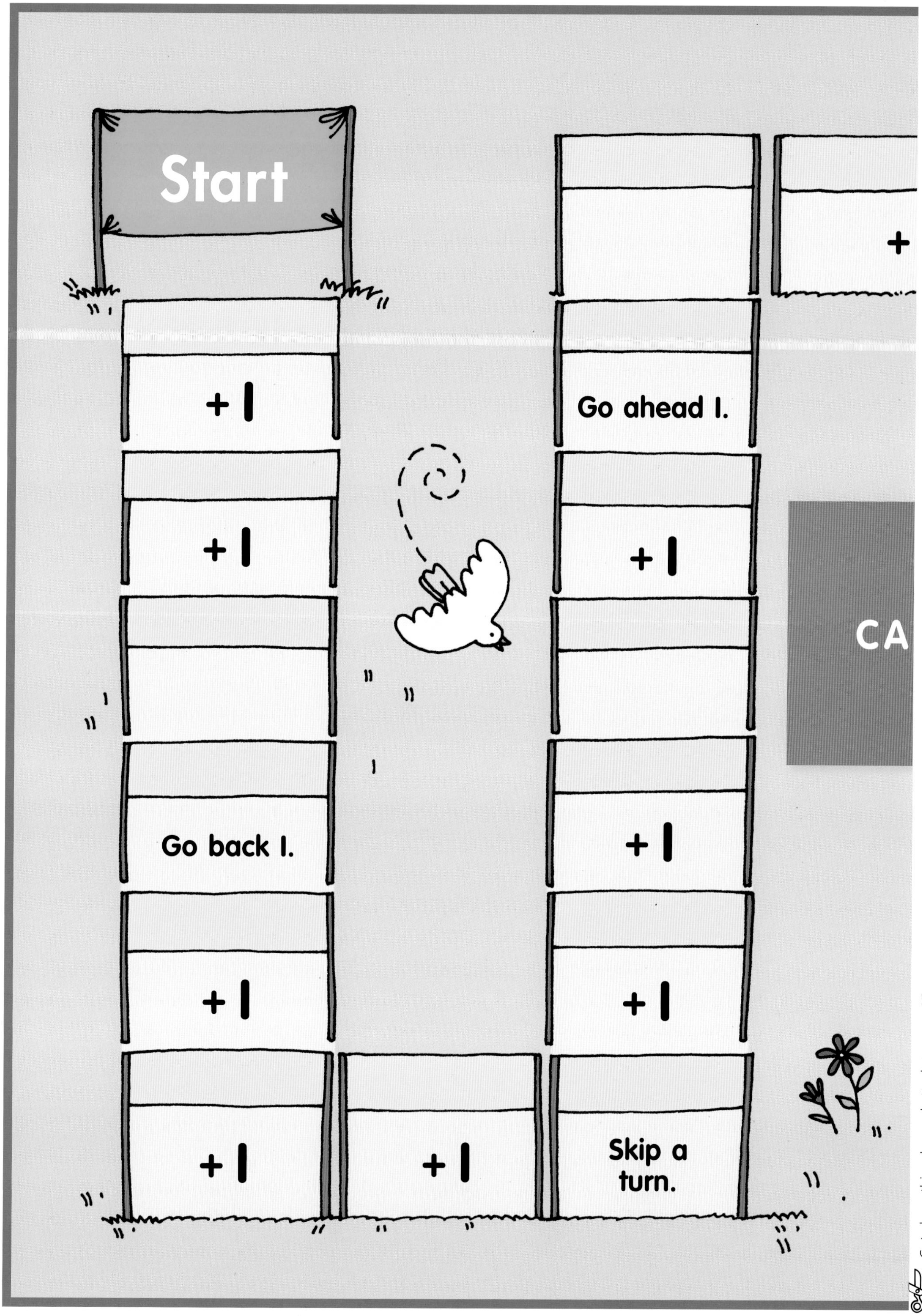
Start
+ 1
+ 1
Go back 1.
+ 1
+ 1
+ 1
Skip a turn.
+ 1
+ 1
+ 1
Go ahead 1.
+
CA

Cut along this edge and attach to page 87.

Finish

+I

Go again.

+I

+I

+I

Go back I.

+I

+I

Go ahead I.

+I

+I

+I

RDS

Finish

+I

+I

Go again.

+I

Go ahead I.

+I

+I

+I

+I

Go back I.

+I

RDS

Cut along this edge and attach to page 85.

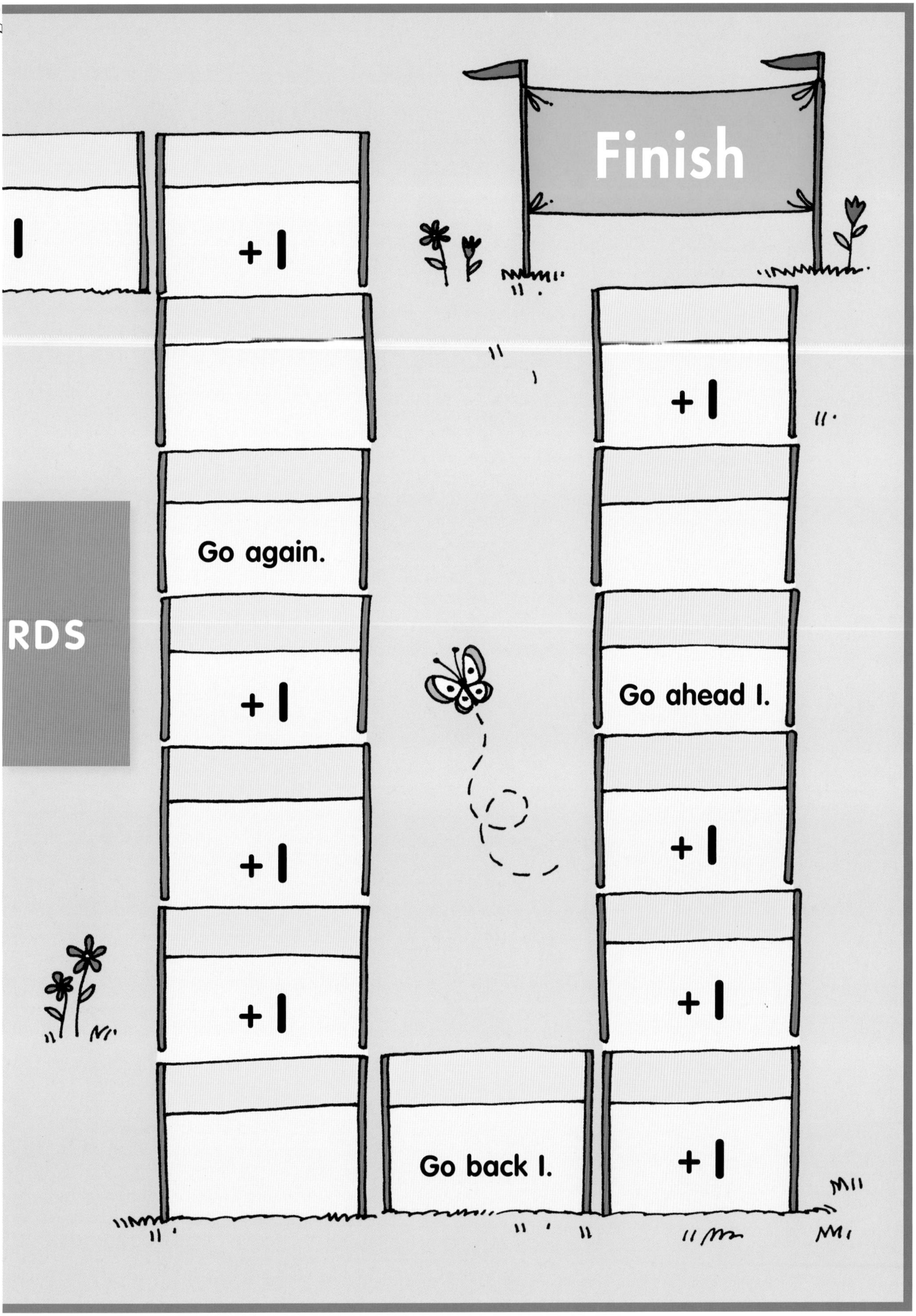

Hippo Hurdles Game Board (right side), page 87

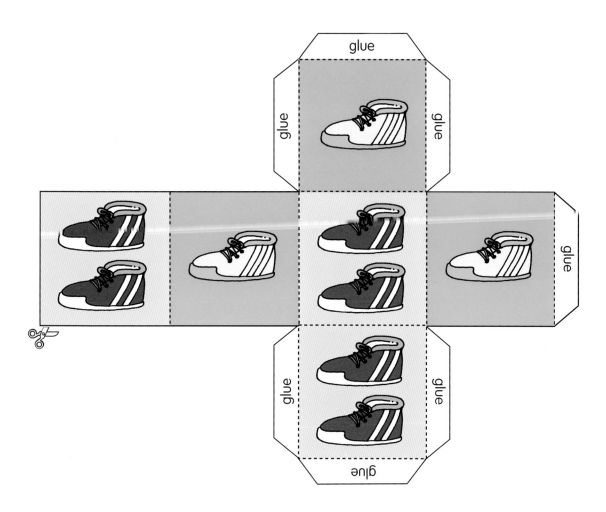

Fold the tabs on the game markers
so they stand up.

Fold here.

Fold here.

Fold here.

Assemble the cube by folding as shown. Glue closed.

Pet Shop

 SKILL

This game provides practice in identifying odd and even numbers.

INTRODUCTION

Show children groups of 1–10 objects, such as crayons, paper clips, one-inch cubes, and so on. Ask them to count the objects and then tell whether the number is odd or even. Help children understand the difference between odd and even numbers.

ASSEMBLING THE GAME

1 Remove pages 93–103 from the book along the perforated lines. Cut out the file-folder label and pocket from page 93. Glue the label onto the file-folder tab. Tape the sides and bottom of the pocket to the front of the folder.

2 Cut out the directions, answer key, and game cards on pages 95 and 97. Place each set of game cards in a separate zipper storage bag. When the game is not in use, store these items in the pocket on the front of the folder.

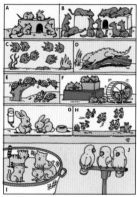

3 Cut out the two sides of the game board on pages 99 and 101 and glue them to the inside of the folder.

4 Cut out and assemble the game cube on page 103.

EXTENDING THE GAME

◎ Invite children to take turns rolling the game cube. Have them read what the cube lands on: Odd or Even. Challenge them to find three numbers around the room that are that kind of number.

◎ Make up simple word problems for children to solve using only even addends or odd addends in each problem. For example, you might say, "Steven bought 4 goldfish. His dad gave him 2 more fish. How many fish does Steven have?" After children solve the problem, ask them to tell whether the answer is an odd or even number.

Pet Shop

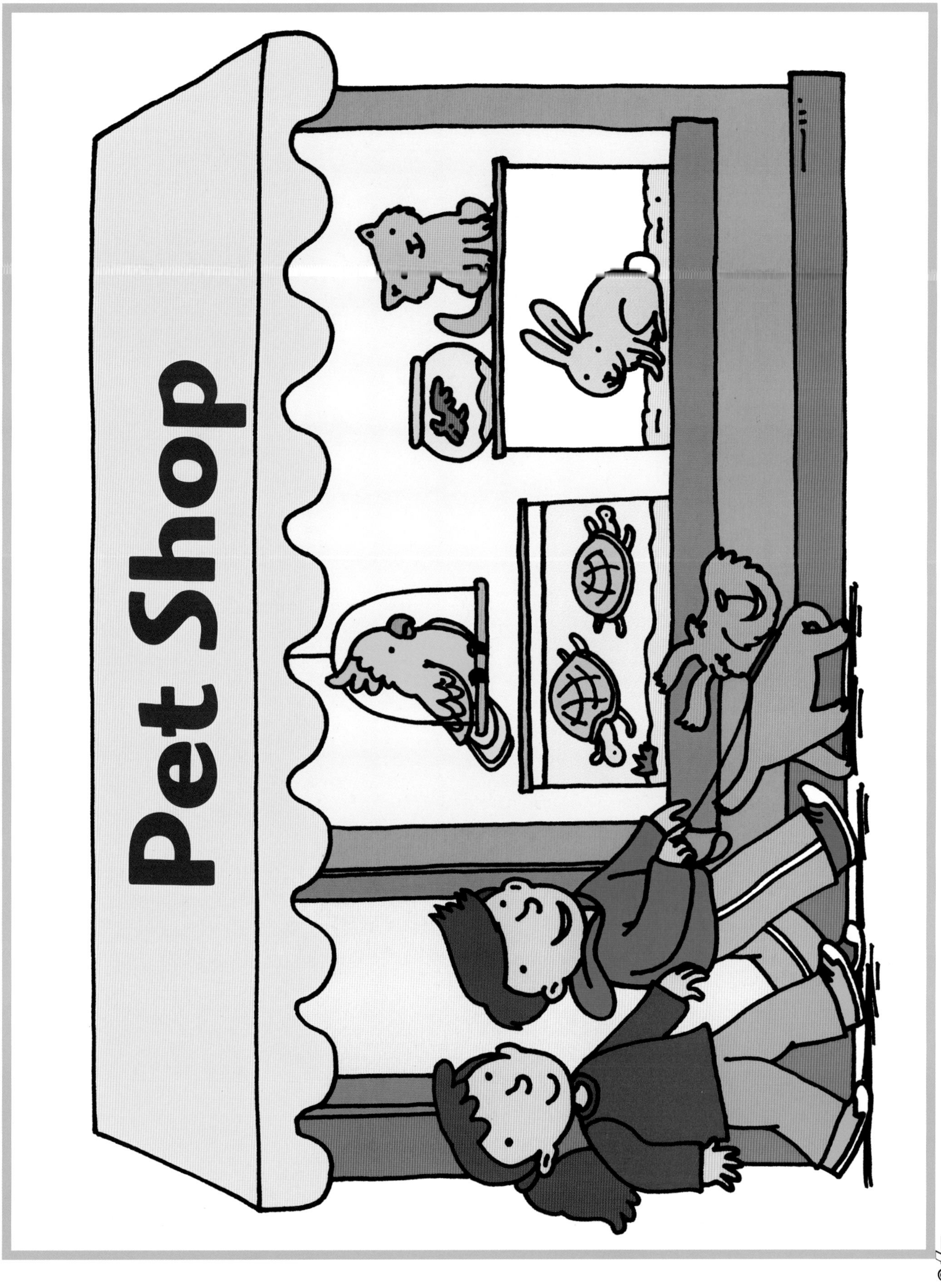

Pet Shop

GET READY TO PLAY

Each player chooses a game board and a set of Sold! cards.

TO PLAY

1 Roll the game cube.

- Did you roll Even? If so, find an even set of animals on your game board. Place a Sold! card on the animals.

- Did you roll Odd? If so, find an odd set of animals on your game board. Place a Sold! card on the animals.

2 Check the answer key. Is your answer correct? If not, take the card back.

3 Keep taking turns. The first player to cover all of his or her animals wins the game.

Pet Shop

ANSWER KEY

Game Board 1

A: even	F: odd
B: odd	G: odd
C: even	H: even
D: even	I: odd
E: odd	J: even

Game Board 2

A: odd	F: even
B: odd	G: even
C: odd	H: even
D: odd	I: even
E: even	J: odd

Sold!	Sold!	Sold!	Sold!
Sold!	Sold!	Sold!	Sold!
Sold!	Sold!	Sold!	Sold!
Sold!	Sold!	Sold!	Sold!
Sold!	Sold!	Sold!	Sold!
Sold!	Sold!	Sold!	Sold!

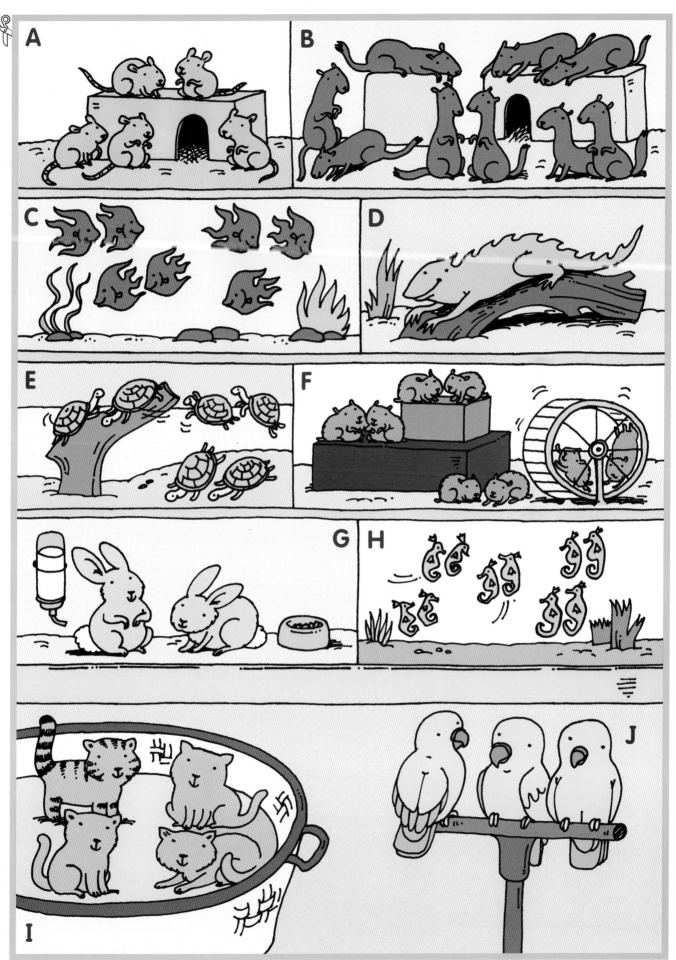

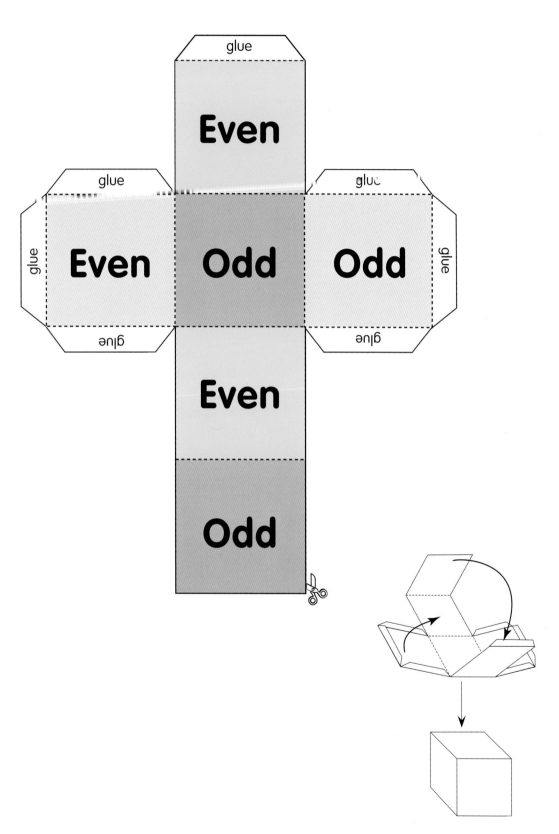

glue

Even

glue   glue

glue **Even** **Odd** **Odd** glue

glue   glue

Even

Odd

Assemble the cube by folding as shown. Glue closed.

Pecking Order

PLAYERS: 2

SKILL

This game provides practice in working with the ordinal numbers 1st–10th.

INTRODUCTION

Display a set of chick cards in random order. Ask children to work together to put the chicks in order from 1st through 10th. Then help them brainstorm things they do in order, such as following directions, passing from one grade to another in school, and lining up to take turns. You might also demonstrate how each ordinal number can be written: as a digit (1st, 2nd and 3rd) or a word (*first, second,* and *third*).

ASSEMBLING THE GAME

1. Remove pages 107–117 from the book along the perforated lines. Cut out the file-folder label and pocket from page 107. Glue the label onto the file-folder tab. Tape the sides and bottom of the pocket to the front of the folder.

2. Cut out the directions, answer key, and game cards on pages 109 and 111. When the game is not in use, store these items in the pocket on the front of the folder.

3. Cut out the two sides of the game board on pages 113 and 115 and glue them to the inside of the folder.

4. Cut out and assemble the game cube on page 117.

EXTENDING THE GAME

◎ Use the game cards to play Memory. Shuffle and place the cards facedown. Then invite children to take turns flipping over two cards at a time to find the matching ordinal numbers. The player with the most matches wins.

◎ Give a pair of children a set of 10 chick cards. Have one child sequence the cards, leaving two or three cards out of the sequence. Challenge the child's partner to name the missing ordinal numbers and then place the corresponding cards in the sequence.

Pecking Order

GET READY TO PLAY

- Each player chooses a hen yard on the game board.
- Shuffle the cards. Stack them facedown.

TO PLAY

1 Roll the game cube. Take that number of cards. Say the ordinal number on each card. Does one of the cards say **1st**?
  - If so, place the card on the first dish on the left side of your hen yard.
  - If not, put all the cards on the bottom of the stack.

2 If you covered the first dish, check any other cards you have.
  - Put the cards on your dishes in order from **1st** to **10th**.
  - Put the cards you can't use on the bottom of the stack.

3 After each turn, check the answer key. Is each answer correct? If not, put that card on the bottom of the stack.

4 Keep taking turns. The first player to cover all of his or her dishes wins the game.

PLAYING TIP

Players may play more than one card on each turn.

Pecking Order

ANSWER KEY

Top hen yard:

Bottom hen yard:

Cut along this edge and attach to page 115.

Cut along this edge and attach to page 113.

Pecking Order Game Board (right side), page 115

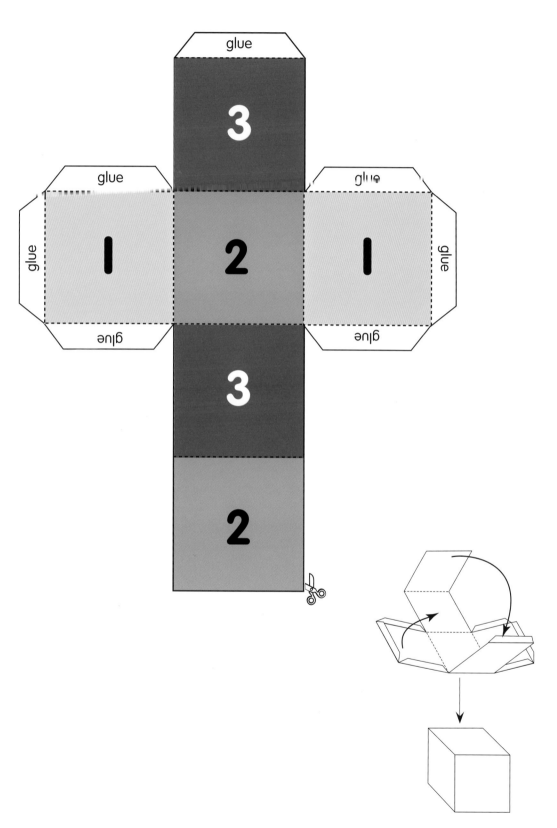

glue

3

glue   glue   glue

1   **2**   **1**

glue   glue   glue

3

2

Assemble the cube by folding as shown. Glue closed.

Leap Frog

SKILL

This game provides practice in skip-counting by 2s up to 20.

INTRODUCTION

Invite children to help you put a set of the frogs in numerical order. When finished, explain that the frogs are ordered by increments of two. Demonstrate how to skip-count by 2s, pointing to the number on the frogs as you count. Repeat several times to give children additional practice in skip-counting by 2s.

ASSEMBLING THE GAME

1 Remove pages 121–129 from the book along the perforated lines. Cut out the file-folder label and pocket from page 121. Glue the label onto the file-folder tab. Tape the sides and bottom of the pocket to the front of the folder.

2 Cut out the directions, answer key, and game cards on pages 123 and 125. When the game is not in use, store these items in the pocket on the front of the folder.

3 Cut out the two game boards on pages 127 and 129 and glue them to the inside of the folder.

EXTENDING THE GAME

◎ Ask children to group small objects into sets of two. Have them make at least 10 sets of 2. Then have children practice skip-counting by pointing to each set as they count.

◎ Brainstorm with children the different body parts that come in pairs, such as hands, legs, eyes, and ears. Then have small groups line up. Name a body part that comes in pairs and have the class count how many are in that group of children. Encourage them to skip-count by 2s to find the result.

Leap Frog

GET READY TO PLAY

- Each player chooses a game board.
- Shuffle the cards. Stack them facedown.

TO PLAY

1 Pick a card and read the number. Is the number a **2**?

- If so, put the card on the first lily pad on your game board. Pick another card.
- If not, put the card on the bottom of the stack.

2 Did you pick another card? Does it have the next number you need to skip-count by 2s? If so, put the card on the next lily pad.

3 Check the answer key. Is your answer correct?

- If so, leave the card on the game board. Then pick another card and go again.
- If not, put the card on the bottom of the stack.

4 Keep taking turns. The first player to cover all of his or her lily pads wins the game.

Leap Frog

ANSWER KEY

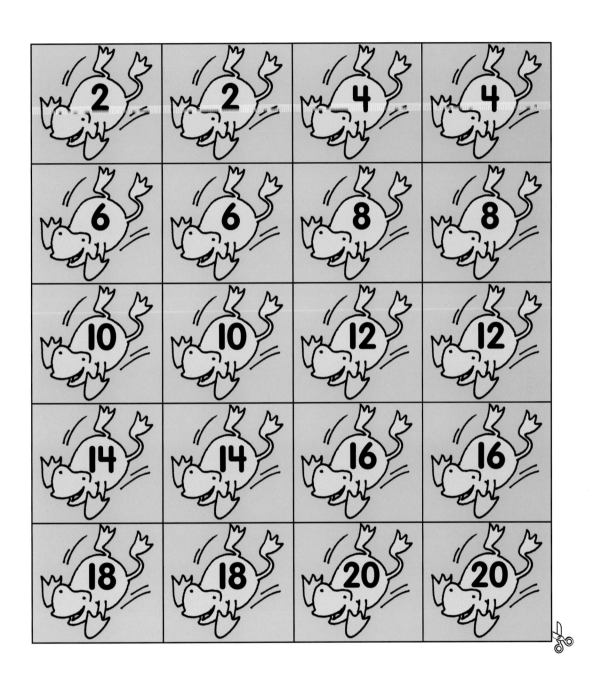

In the Doghouse

PLAYERS: 2

SKILL This game provides practice in matching numbers to number words.

INTRODUCTION

Review with children the number words for 1–10: *one, two, three, four, five, six, seven, eight, nine,* and *ten.* Write each word on the chalkboard. Then, using one set of game cards, show children one number at a time. Have them find the matching number word on the board.

ASSEMBLING THE GAME

1 Remove pages 133–143 from the book along the perforated lines. Cut out the file-folder label and pocket from page 133. Glue the label onto the file-folder tab. Tape the sides and bottom of the pocket to the front of the folder.

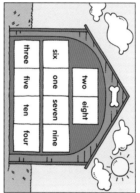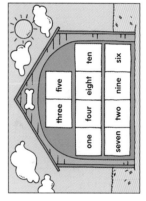

2 Cut out the directions, answer key, and game cards on pages 135 and 137. Place each set of game cards in a separate zipper storage bag. When the game is not in use, store these items in the pocket on the front of the folder.

3 Cut out the two game boards on pages 139 and 141 and glue them to the inside of the folder.

4 Cut out and assemble the game spinner on page 143.

EXTENDING THE GAME

◎ Write each number from 1–10 on a separate index card. Repeat for the number words. Then invite children to use the cards to play Memory. Have them try to find the matching numbers and number words.

◎ Ask each child to cover all the boxes on his or her game board with dog cards. Then have the children take turns removing one card at a time, reading the number word, and then finding a matching number in print around the room.

In the Doghouse

In the Doghouse

GET READY TO PLAY

Each player chooses a game board and a set of 10 dog cards.

TO PLAY

1. Spin the spinner. Name the number it lands on.
   Do you have that number word on your game board?
   - If so, put a dog card on the word.
   - If not, your turn ends.

2. After each turn, check the answer key. Is your answer correct?
   If not, take the card back.

3. Keep taking turns. The first player to cover all of his or her
   boxes wins the game.

PLAYING TIP

Players may put only one card on each number word.

In the Doghouse

ANSWER KEY

one: 1	six: 6
two: 2	seven: 7
three: 3	eight: 8
four: 4	nine: 9
five: 5	ten: 10

three

six

five

one

ten

seven

four

nine

two

eight

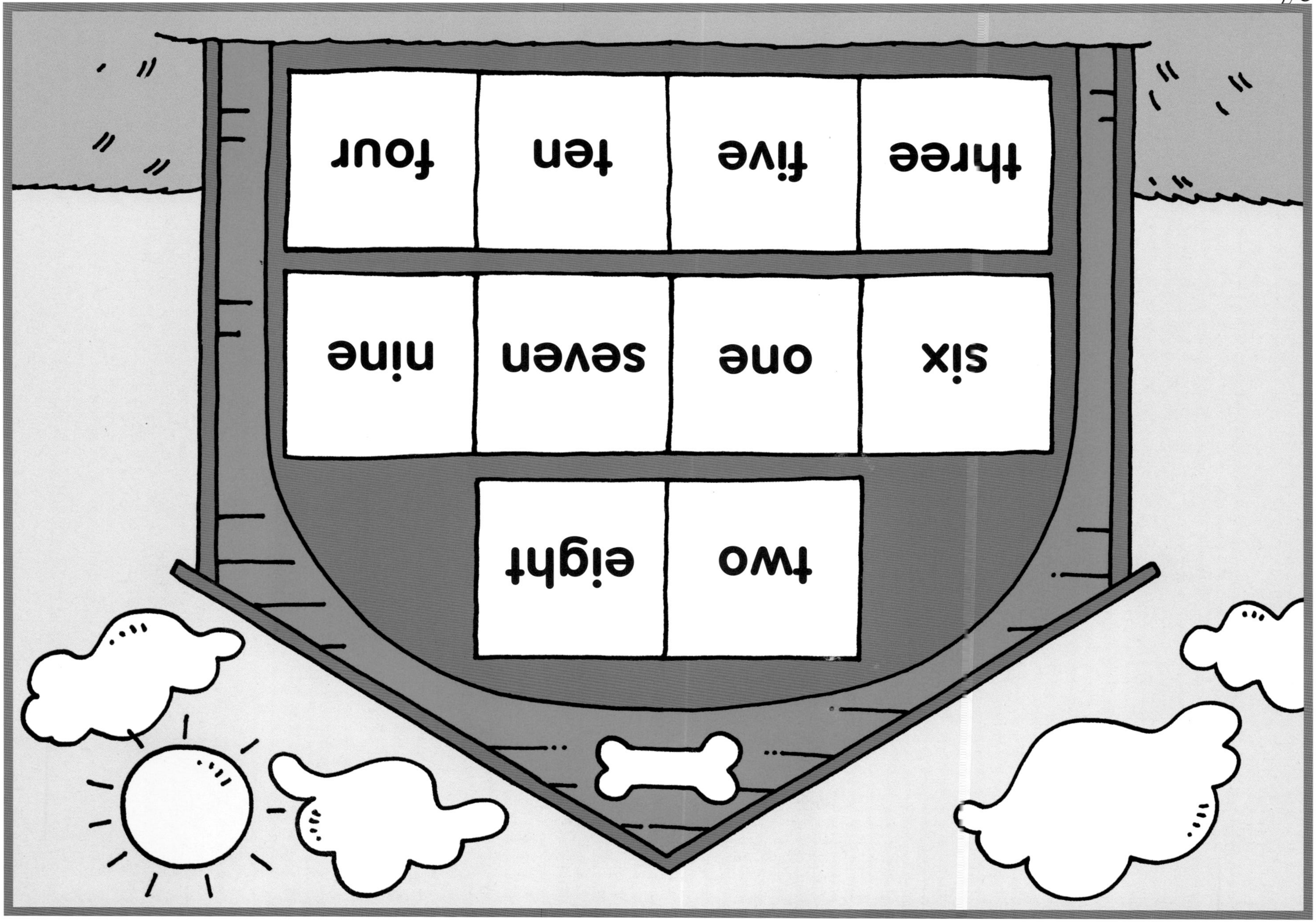

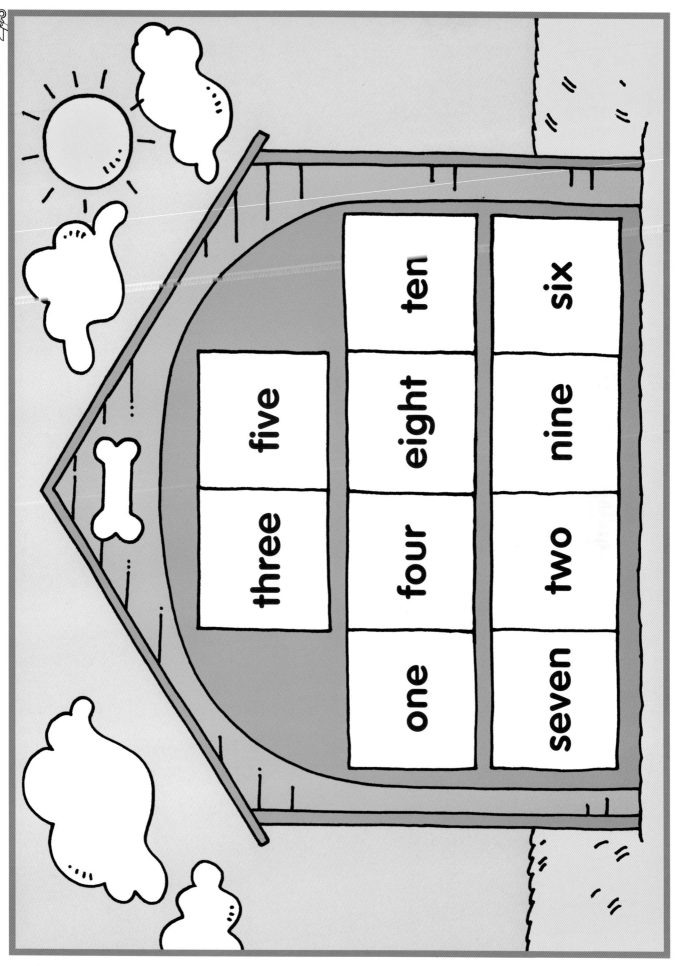

brass fastener

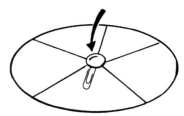

Assemble the spinner using a paper clip and brass fastener as shown. Make sure the paper clip spins easily.